by Greg Long

Illustrated by Nathan Wondrak

Halo
Publishing International
www.halopublishing.com

For more information, contact: laughalongbooks.com
Email Author at: greglong@laughalongbooks.com

Library of Congress Control Number: 2010902200
ISBN 978-1-935268-23-9

Halo
Publishing International
www.halopublishing.com

Printed in China

I would like to thank the Three who made this possible—
God - The Father, God - The Son, and God - The Holy Ghost.
Lord, I am Thine.

A Special Thanks to my lovely wife, Sean Marie—
You are God's gift to me from Heaven and my Earthly inspiration.
Siempre Juntos.

I also would like to thank...
Little Girl, Ben, Douglas, and Lulu— I love my pack!
Mom and Dad—you gave me the foundation that weathered the storms of doubt.
The Captain and Elda—you helped us keep the dream alive.
All my wonderful family and friends who kept us in their prayers.

And thank you PY.

-Greg

I must thank God because He used this book as a part of His plan to get me
through a hard part of my life.

Second, I want to thank the author of *Today I Found God*, Greg Long, for not only
trusting me to illustrate his first book, but also for the patience he had during all
the ups and downs it took to create the art.

Finally, I want to thank my parents for simply being supportive of my artistic life
and raising me with God.

-Nathan

This morning at breakfast I dropped all the eggs.
I then dropped the bacon and burned both my legs.

I spilled a whole gallon of paint on the floor.
When cleaning it up, I spilled even more.

I lost the five dollars my uncle gave me.

My frisbee got stuck
at the top of a tree.

I'm s'posed to go fishing,
but can't find my rod--

"I've been really good. (At least I have tried.)

I know I am blessed because Jesus died.

So why are You making me have a bad day?

Answer me now; I must know right away."

I wait--- but no answer.
That makes me sad.
Pretty soon God's
silence is making me mad!

"Answer me, God!
I'm talking to You!
If You keep this up,
here's what I will do—
I'll come and I'll find You
and make You explain
the reason You're making
me go through this pain."

I wait a bit longer. Nope— not a word.

I know He can hear me. I know that He heard.

God probably thinks I'll just give up and cry,

so I will show Him He picked on the wrong guy.

I'll find Him and make Him tell all that He knows.

If He doesn't answer, I'll stomp on His toes.

I hop on my bike and begin my God search.
I know where to find Him— I'll find Him at church.

I pedal real fast. This shouldn't take long.

He thinks I won't find Him, I'll show Him He's wrong.

I get to the church, and I jump off my bike. I burst through the door, and then I am like,

"Hey, God, it's me— the kid You ignore. I don't want You picking on me anymore."

I look all around, but no one is there.

God must be hiding, the question is "Where?"

Not under the pew,

or by the window,

or behind the altar,

or– "Yipes! Uh-Hello."

"Hello, right back at you,"
laughs Pastor Chuck.
"You look like a kid
who is down on his luck.
Is there something in here
you're trying to find?
What's troubling you, son?
What's on your mind?"

"Actually, Pastor,

I'm root-tootin' mad,

'cause God's made this

day so incredibly bad.

He won't answer me

when I call out His name.

So, where's He hiding?

I'm sick of this game."

Pastor Chuck nods his head, then says, "I see

I'd be mad too if that happened to me.

So that's why it hurts me to tell you the news—

You probably won't find Him under the pews.

If you want to find God, don't start your search here.

You need to start looking a little more near."

"More near? Like my house? Or in my backyard?

Maybe my search for God won't be that hard.

Who knows, today might change into a fun day.

Thanks, Pastor Chuck. I'll see you on Sunday."

I jump on my bike, and laugh while I'm riding.

God thinks He's smart, but I'll find where He's hiding.

I get to my house and I search all around.

It shouldn't be long until He is found.

If I were God, now where would I be?

He's not in the car, or up in a tree,

or in the garage, or out in the garden,

or under Dad's shirt— "Oops,

I beg your pardon."

I'm starting to think that God must be inside. There are lots of good places in there to hide.

He's not in the closet,
or inside the vent,

or behind the sofa,
or in the basement.

He's not in the bathtub
or under the sink.
Where could He be?
Come on, Think-Think-Think!

There must be someplace
I haven't looked yet--
some dark secret place
that most people forget.

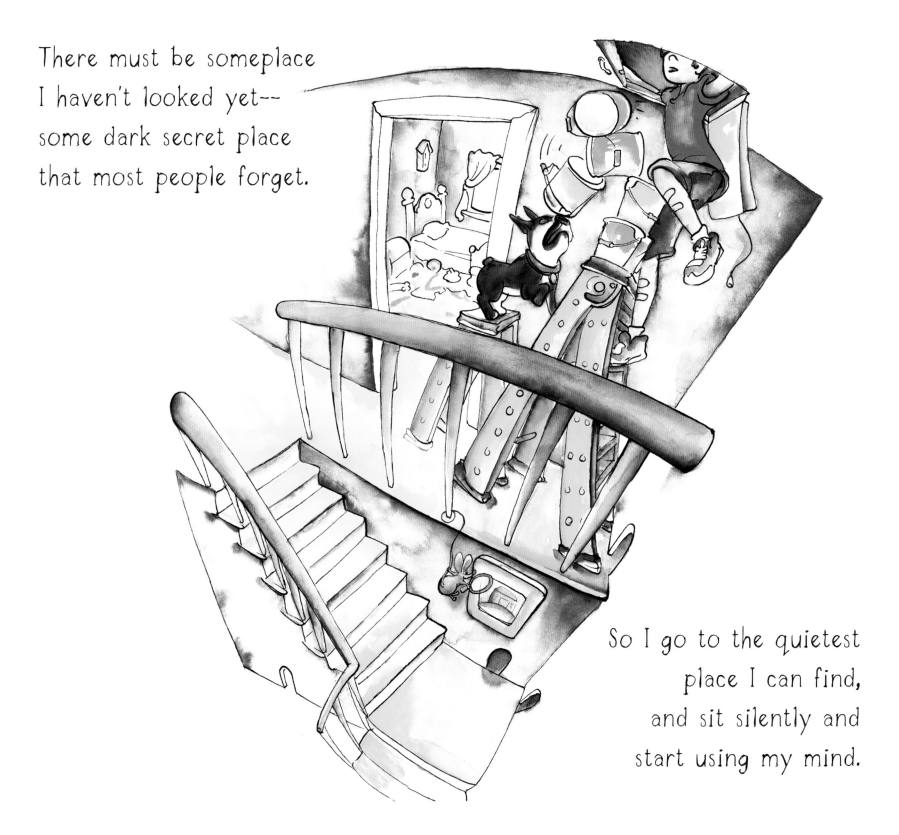

So I go to the quietest
place I can find,
and sit silently and
start using my mind.

I think about God, and where He might be,

and that's when I hear God's voice inside of me.

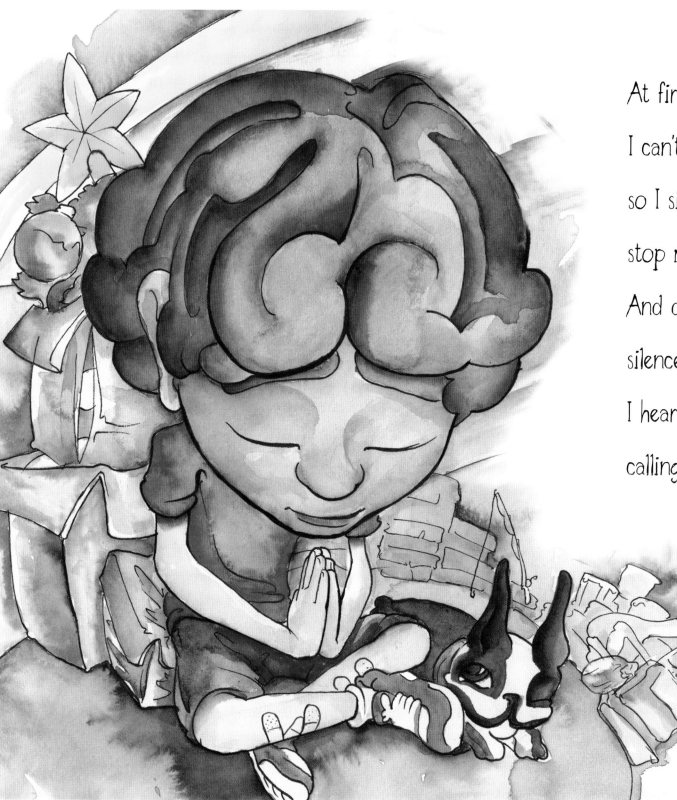

At first it's so quiet
I can't make it out,
so I sit very still and
stop moving about.
And deep in that
silence that I feel within
I hear God's voice
calling to me again.

God says, "I am here; I have always been here.

I am always with you; I am always near.

I'm sorry your day has been bad, but please know

I let these bad things happen so you will grow.

In every misfortune there hides something great.

Sometimes it comes quickly; sometimes you must wait.

So trust in Me always-- we're never apart.

Whenever you need Me, I'm here in your heart."

After God speaks I feel touched by His grace,

and can't seem to wipe this big grin from my face.

I want to yell out to the world "Hey, it's true—

God's really inside me; He's really in you!

He's in everything— you just have to look,

and— Ouch! What's that? I'm stuck on a hook!"

I tug on the hook— and I find my lost rod.

But I found so much more, 'cause today I found God.